TABLE OF CONTENTS

ASIANA AIRLINES FLIGHT 214

July 6, 2013, was a beautiful summer day at San Francisco International Airport. The sun was shining and there was a light breeze. Visibility looked good for Asiana Airlines Flight 214, which had flown from South Korea. The control tower had given the pilots clearance to land the huge Boeing 777 passenger jet. The flight's 291 passengers and 12 flight attendants were buckled in their seats. The ten-hour nonstop flight was finally coming to an end.

Disaster Science

The Science of
a Plane Crash

Carol S. Surges

Published in the United States of America by Cherry Lake Publishing
Ann Arbor, Michigan
www.cherrylakepublishing.com

Consultants: Jeffrey C. Price, Associate Professor, Department of Aviation & Aerospace Science, Metropolitan State University of Denver; Marla Conn, ReadAbility, Inc.
Editorial direction: Red Line Editorial
Book design and illustration: Design Lab

Photo Credits: Marcio Jose Sanchez/AP Images, cover, 1, 8; Anatoliy Lukich/Shutterstock Images, 5; Jeff Chiu/AP Images, 7; Evan Vucci/AP Images, 11; US Air Force, 13; Dorling Kindersley/Thinkstock, 15, 20; Frank May/dpa/Corbis, 18; Jason DeCrow/AP Images, 22; Brazil's Air Force/AP Images, 25; Mark Lennihan/AP Images, 28

Library of Congress Cataloging-in-Publication Data
Surges, Carol S., author.
  The science of a plane crash / by Carol S. Surges.
    pages cm. -- (Disaster science)
  Audience: Age 11.
  Audience: Grades 4 to 6.
  Includes bibliographical references and index.
  ISBN 978-1-63137-626-9 (hardcover) -- ISBN 978-1-63137-671-9 (pbk.) -- ISBN 978-1-63137-716-7 (pdf ebook) -- ISBN 978-1-63137-761-7 (hosted ebook)
  1. Aircraft accidents--Investigation--Juvenile literature. 2. Aeronautics--Juvenile literature. I. Title.

  TL553.5.S755 2015
  363.12'465--dc23   2014004032

Cherry Lake Publishing would like to acknowledge the work of
The Partnership for 21st Century Skills. Please visit www.p21.org
for more information.

Printed in the United States of America
Corporate Graphics Inc.
July 2014

ABOUT THE AUTHOR

At one time, Carol S. Surges took the Federal Aviation Administration test to be an air traffic controller. She made it all the way to the physical, where her poor depth perception changed her plans. Instead, she returned to working in a school library, teaching science and flying whenever she gets the chance.

Boeing 777s had an excellent safety record.

Inside the **cockpit**, things were not looking as good.
When the pilots dropped below 200 feet (60 m), they
likely noticed the plane was going too slowly and their
altitude was falling too quickly. The plane was heading
into a **stall**, a situation in which an aircraft is going so
slowly it cannot be controlled. In order to avoid this, the

pilots may have tried to lower the plane's nose and increase its speed. But according to early reports, the pilots of Flight 214 reacted too late.

The jet's tail struck the seawall, a barrier that separates the airport from San Francisco Bay. The tail section was ripped off while the rest of the plane slid down the **runway**, scattering parts along the way. By the time the plane came to a stop on the grass next to the runway, it had spun almost completely around. A fire soon broke out in the **cabin** and the crew gave the order to evacuate the plane. Rescue workers rushed to the scene.

Incredibly, there were only two immediate deaths from the crash. Two teenagers died when the plane's tail was ripped off. A third person died after the crash. She was a teenager buried under a layer of foam used by aircraft firefighters. She died when she was hit by a fire truck.

At first glance, nothing about the flight indicated a risk of a crash. The pilots that day were highly trained

Despite terrible damage to the plane, nearly every person on board survived.

with many hours of experience. Boeing 777 jets had never been involved in a fatal crash before. They were equipped with all the latest technology and safety gear. The weather was good, and the runway was well maintained.

So why did Asiana Airlines Flight 214 crash that Saturday morning? Exactly what happened and how did it happen? Those are the questions that investigators work to answer after every airplane crash. In order to do this, they study every piece of evidence, interview people involved in the accident, and test their **hypotheses** until they can answer why the crash happened.

After the disaster, investigators worked carefully to understand why the plane had crashed.

INVESTIGATIONS

The National Transportation Safety Board (NTSB), the Federal Aviation Administration (FAA), and sometimes the Federal Bureau of Investigation (FBI) study airplane crashes in the United States. They look at the crash from every possible perspective in order to understand exactly what happened. They examine the cockpit voice recorder and flight data recorder. These durable devices, also known as the black boxes despite the fact that they are orange in color, record what happens on a flight and are designed to survive crashes. Every piece of wreckage is studied. Survivors and witnesses are interviewed, and the plane's flight and maintenance history are reviewed. When the investigation is done, investigators issue a detailed report. The report includes the likely causes of the accident and a list of recommendations to improve safety on future flights.

CHAPTER 2

FORCES ADD UP

Investigations always begin at the crash site. Parts of the plane are examined and carefully documented. Back in labs and offices, investigators study these parts, as well as data from the flight. They carry out tests and computer **simulations**. Eventually, all the findings are put together to describe the series of events leading up to the disaster. These events are known as the accident chain.

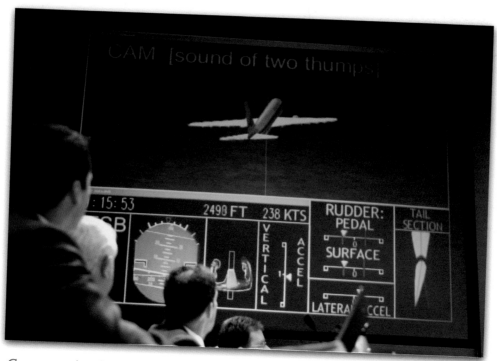

CAM [sound of two thumps]

: 15: 53
CB
2490 FT   238 KTS
VERTICAL
ACCEL
RUDDER:
PEDAL
TAIL
SECTION
SURFACE
LATERAL CCEL

Computer simulations can help investigators make sense of complex information.

Before discussing how an airplane crashes, it is important to understand how it flies. There are four forces that must be controlled during flight. They are weight, lift, thrust, and drag. Keeping these forces in balance is what keeps airplanes in the sky. The study of how objects move through air and interact with these forces is known as aerodynamics.

The most obvious force an airplane deals with is weight. Gravity pulls objects toward Earth, giving those objects weight. Airplanes must overcome gravity's pull in order to fly. Because objects with more mass are pulled with more force, larger planes must work harder to overcome gravity.

Lift is an upward pushing force that helps airplanes counteract the downward pull of gravity. Airplane wings are designed to create lift. When in motion, their shape causes air to move more quickly over the top of the wing than under the bottom of the wing. This results in lower pressure above the wing than below it, forcing the wing to move upward into the lower pressure area. This makes it possible for airplanes to fly. Pointing the plane up or down changes the amount of lift the wings generate. Lift also changes at different speeds and altitudes.

Like lift, thrust is a pushing force. Airplane engines create thrust to push the plane forward. As the plane moves faster, the air moving across the airplane's wings also moves faster and lift increases. When lift is stronger than the pull of gravity, the plane begins to fly.

The Four Forces

This diagram shows the four forces that act on an airplane. Think about the effect of any of these forces going out of balance. For example, what would happen if the force of thrust increased? How would this affect the other forces?

Thrust

Lift

Weight

Drag

Lift

Weight is not the only pulling force during flight. Drag is the fourth force of flight. Drag is also known as air resistance. The air that a plane flies through pushes against the plane in the opposite direction of its motion. Airplanes are designed to minimize drag forces. This is why they often have sleek, smooth surfaces. This makes it easier for air to move past the plane, rather than push against it. The more drag a plane encounters, the more thrust it needs to move forward. During landings, pilots use parts of the wings called flaps to increase drag, slowing the plane down.

The wrong amount of force at the wrong time can cause accidents. Balancing the four forces is the challenge of safe flight. For Asiana Airlines Flight 214, the plane lost lift as its speed decreased too quickly. The pull of gravity overpowered the plane and slammed its tail into the seawall.

THE PARTS OF AN AIRPLANE

This diagram points out important parts of an airplane and their functions. Think about what would happen if one of these parts failed. In what way would the airplane be more difficult to control? How might a failure of one or more parts lead to a crash?

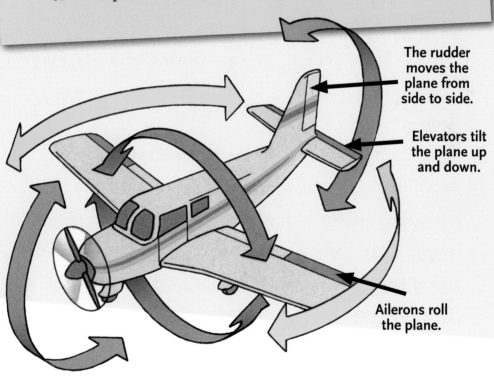

The rudder moves the plane from side to side.

Elevators tilt the plane up and down.

Ailerons roll the plane.

How Planes Crash

Fatal plane crashes are incredibly rare. More than 8.9 million airline flights took off within the United States in 2012. Not a single one had a fatal crash. When crashes do happen, it is because the four forces of flight are somehow thrown out of balance. Several different factors can contribute to this imbalance. Design flaws, bad weather, collisions, and simple pilot error can all lead to a crash.

THE FIRST PLANE CRASH

Orville and Wilbur Wright designed and built the first airplane in 1903. During a demonstration flight in 1908, Orville Wright lost control of his plane and it crashed nose first from about 100 feet (30 m). Wright had broken bones, but his passenger was not so lucky. He died the next day. The Wrights learned from the crash and continued to make improvements to their planes.

Even a minor error in the design of an airplane can result in a disaster. On October 24, 1947, United Airlines Flight 608 was traveling from Los Angeles to Chicago. The aircraft was a Douglas DC-6, a four-engine plane capable of carrying approximately 100 passengers. A few hours into the flight, a fire broke out in the baggage compartment. Smoke filled the plane. The pilots tried to land, but the plane crashed on the way to the nearest airport. There were no survivors. Investigators immediately tried to discover what had gone wrong.

They found that the DC-6 had a fuel vent near a device that sucked in air to heat the cabin. If fuel leaked from the vent, it could get sucked into the heating device. Testing on the ground showed that this could lead to a fire if it happened while the cabin heater was

The DC-6 used propellers instead of faster, more modern jet engines.

turned on. After the investigation, all DC-6 aircraft were grounded and modified to prevent another disaster.

Weather conditions called microbursts are dangerous to airplanes. Microbursts are sudden, powerful gusts of wind that move downward from storm clouds and travel outward when they hit the ground. When they happen during takeoff or landing, the quick shift in winds, known as wind shear, can cause a crash.

This is what happened to Delta Air Lines Flight 191 on August 2, 1985. The three-engine Lockheed L-1011 passenger jet was traveling from Fort Lauderdale, Florida, to the Dallas/Fort Worth International Airport in Texas. As they prepared to land, the pilots noticed potentially dangerous storms in their path but did not try to avoid them. The airplane got caught in a microburst less than 1,000 feet (300 m) above the ground.

The pilots tried to speed up, increase altitude, and fly around for another landing attempt, but it was too late. The plane struck the ground before reaching the

Planes can usually fly safely through storms, but pilots must still use caution.

runway, hitting a car on a highway and killing the driver. The left wing then hit a structure at the airport, causing the aircraft to spin counterclockwise and explode. Of the 163 people on board, only 29 survived. An investigation showed that the weather conditions, as well as the pilots' failure to avoid the storm, led to the crash.

Midair collisions with objects are another cause of plane crashes. The biggest risks happen during takeoff and landing. One of the most serious dangers is known as bird strike. This happens when a bird collides with an airplane or gets sucked into its engine. One of the most famous examples of a bird strike happened to US Airways Flight 1549 on January 15, 2009. The airplane involved was a two-engine Airbus A320 jet. The flight was scheduled to travel from New York City to Charlotte, North Carolina.

The journey was cut short just minutes into the flight. At around 3,000 feet (900 m), both engines lost power. When a burning smell filled the cockpit, the pilot knew there had been a bird strike. But the plane did not have enough thrust to return to the airport. Instead, the pilot aimed for the Hudson River. Airline pilots are trained for water landings, but having to perform one is extremely rare. The pilot of Flight 1549, Chesley Sullenberger, was highly skilled. He brought the plane down safely. The passengers and crew were soon rescued by nearby boats. No one died.

Captain Sullenberger, shown here in front of a photo of his amazing landing, became a national hero.

INVESTIGATING FLIGHT 427

When USAir Flight 427 crashed near Pittsburgh, Pennsylvania, on September 8, 1994, 132 people died. The NTSB began an investigation of the Boeing 737 crash immediately. Multiple theories about its cause were tested, but investigators could not agree on the problem. Many people believed the **rudder** system had failed. The rudder, a control surface on the tail, allows the plane to change its side-to-side direction. The power control unit (PCU) that moved the rudder was taken apart, x-rayed, and inspected piece by piece. No problems were found.

Finally, in 1996, investigators met to look at the evidence again. They thought the PCU might have failed because of cold temperatures during flight. This time, tests were done using the same temperature conditions found at high altitudes. The PCU from Flight 427 was tested alongside a brand-new one. During the tests, the PCU from the plane that crashed kept jamming while the new one worked. But the **engineers** noticed something troubling. Under some conditions, a small jam could cause the rudder control to reverse. A pilot could move the controls to the left, and the rudder would instead steer the plane to the right. More tests confirmed the problem. Boeing redesigned the system to prevent jams. The investigation showed that thorough testing could reveal the causes of crashes, even if they were as minor as a jam in a rudder control system.

STOPPING THE ACCIDENT CHAIN

On June 1, 2009, Air France Flight 447 headed toward a monster thunderstorm. The flight would soon go on record as France's deadliest air disaster. The accident chain began when the plane flew directly into a storm over the Atlantic Ocean. The plane's wings became covered in ice, causing it to lose lift. A device that prevents stalls stopped working, and the aircraft went into a fatal stall. When the plane's black boxes were finally recovered two years later, the cause of the accident became clear. It was a combination of pilot error, lack of training, and equipment malfunction. These issues, like the causes of most plane crashes, are preventable or avoidable.

Weather can usually be predicted, and pilots are trained to avoid certain kinds of severe weather. Airports

Investigators later recovered the debris from Flight 447 from the ocean.

sometimes even delay flights during bad storms. Pilots review weather patterns before every takeoff, studying weather maps carefully. Most violent weather is located close to the ground. Ice, snow, slush, sleet, and wind bursts can usually be avoided at higher altitudes. Improved training and warning systems also help pilots deal with weather problems. Still, weather can change without notice and **turbulence** can be a problem at cruising altitude.

Before every flight, pilots review other details besides the weather. They walk around their aircraft to check for any issues on the plane's **hull** and other parts. Pilots check the plane's weight and balance to ensure the plane will have enough thrust and lift for flight. They use checklists to take them through the correct steps for takeoff and landing. This attention to detail helps make air travel extremely safe.

Today's planes have back-up systems that help avoid problems. But with hundreds of switches, instruments,

FLIGHT SIMULATORS

Pilots must complete many training hours inside a simulator. This is a model cockpit with realistic controls. Instead of windows, it uses computer screens to show what a pilot would see during a real flight. Some simulators sit on supports that allow them to move, giving them the feel of an actual flight. A simulator operator sits at a computer station. He or she can program different flight situations into the simulator, giving the pilot a chance to train for many different situations.

and warning lights in the cockpit, pilots have a lot to keep track of. It's very rare, but sometimes systems fail. Even with all their training, pilots can miss warnings. Some air travel experts believe that pilots are becoming overly dependent upon automatic systems, and that pilots need additional training on how to fly without these systems.

People have been flying for more than a century. Since the first flights, aircraft designers and pilots have needed to understand the forces that allow planes to move through the air. Today, engineers and scientists

Modern jet cockpits have many screens, buttons, and switches, and flying them safely requires intense training.

study every accident with these forces in mind. After more than 100 years of learning about how planes can fail, the major problems have been fixed. This makes finding the causes of plane crashes more difficult than ever before. Investigators must look at every last detail of the flight, studying and testing every possibility until they find the answer. Thanks to people who investigate crashes, every accident that happens leads to improvements to flight safety.

FIXING THE COMET

The de Havilland Comet was the first commercial jet airliner. Introduced in 1952, the plane could fly higher and faster than most other planes of its time. Every airline wanted one. But then a series of fatal crashes affected the future of jet airliners. Investigators blamed each crash on a different problem. Finally, the planes were grounded.

Investigators decided to try reconstructing one of the planes from the broken pieces to discover why it crashed. This technique had never been used before. It became clear that each crash had resulted from the same problem. Jet aircraft fly at high altitudes where the air is thin. They must be sealed off and filled with thicker air to make the aircraft comfortable for the passengers inside. This process is called pressurizing. Each pressurization weakens the plane's metal body, similar to how a metal paper clip weakens when you bend it repeatedly. The weakening process is known as metal fatigue. Scientists learned more about metal fatigue from the accidents. They changed the design of jet aircraft to make them stronger.

TOP FIVE WORST PLANE CRASHES

1. **March 27, 1977: Tenerife, Canary Islands**
    When two Boeing 747 jumbo jets crashed into each other on the runway, a total of 583 passengers and crew members were killed.

2. **August 12, 1985: Mount Takamagahara, Japan**
    A Boeing 747 had a mechanical error that sent it crashing into Mount Takamagahara. A total of 520 people died in the deadliest single-aircraft accident in history.

3. **November 12, 1996: Near New Delhi, India**
    Shortly after departing from Indira Gandhi International Airport, Saudi Arabian Airlines Flight 763 crashed into incoming Kazakhstan Airlines Flight 1907. A total of 349 victims died in the deadliest midair collision in history.

4. **March 3, 1974: Bois d' Ermenonville, France**
    A chain of events that began when a faulty rear cargo hatch blew off ended with a plane out of control. Turkish Airlines Flight 981 crashed near Paris, France, killing all 346 people on board.

5. **May 25, 1979: Chicago, United States**
    Soon after takeoff, one of the engines on American Airlines Flight 191 detached from the aircraft and damaged a wing, causing the plane to crash. All 273 people on the plane died, along with two more people on the ground.

LEARN MORE

FURTHER READING

Hook, Jason. *In the Air*. Austin, TX: Raintree Steck-Vaughn, 2003.

Laws, Gordon D. and Lauren M. Laws. *Airplane Crashes*. Farmington Hills, MI: Lucent, 2004.

Leavitt, Amie Jane. *Anatomy of a Plane Crash*. Mankato, MN: Capstone, 2011.

Woods, Michael and Mary B. Woods. *Air Disasters*. Minneapolis, MN: Lerner, 2008.

WEB SITES

NASA—Virtual Skies
http://virtualskies.arc.nasa.gov/index.html
This Web site features interesting information on all aspects of air travel, from how airports are designed to how pilots navigate through the skies.

Smithsonian—How Things Fly
http://howthingsfly.si.edu
This Web site has cool videos and animations that show how the forces of flight work.

GLOSSARY

altitude (AL-ti-tood) height above the ground

cabin (KAB-in) the inside of an airplane

cockpit (KOK-pit) the section of an aircraft in which pilots sit

engineers (en-juh-NIHRS) people who use math and science to build things and solve problems

hull (HUHL) the main body of an airplane

hypotheses (hye-POTH-uh-sees) predictions based on evidence

rudder (RUHD-ur) a control surface at the rear of the plane that is used to control the plane's direction

runway (RUHN-way) a flat surface where airplanes land

simulations (sim-yuh-LAY-shuns) tests that represent the conditions likely to happen during a real flight

stall (STAWL) a situation in which there is not enough air traveling over an airplane's wings to generate the lift needed to stay in the air

turbulence (TUR-byuh-luhnce) an air condition that can cause bumpy flights

INDEX

[21ST CENTURY SKILLS LIBRARY]